"Reflections" ...

... for someone special

... all thoughts are originals of :~

    ... Brock Tully

illustrations :~

    ... Heidi Thompson

calligraphy :~

    ... Brock Tully

~Other books by Brock Tully ~
   1. Reflections ~ for living life fully.
   2. Reflections ~ for touching hearts.
   3. Coming Together ~ a 10,000 mile
                     bicycle journey.
   4. With Hope We Can All Find
        Ogo Pogo ~ for the child in us all.
     5. Reflections ~ for sharing dreams.

* printed on recycled paper.

ISBN # 0-9693583-0-X

Dedicated to :~
    Gandhi, Martin Luther King,
    and Winnie-the-Pooh.

Inspiration :~
    ... that beautiful voice
        within us all
        that teaches truth & love...
    ... to those who help us
        stop & listen ...
    ... to those who forgive us
        when we lose touch.

"I'm seeing more & more that life is a
"reflection" of how i'm feeling about myself ...
... to 'grow', for me, has meant making
changes, forgiving myself & others, & staying
in touch with the 'child' that i believe
is within us all ...

... i hope this little book gives you
the support to 'grow' that so many
friends have given to me & ...

... i hope it leaves you thinking,
smiling, & caring a bit more ...

... so we can all 'live' life fully & in peace.

"... i'll never find out
  What i can do...
unless i do all i can
  to find out."

"... the beautiful thing
        about saying 'no' to me ...
... is that when you say 'yes'
        i know you really mean it."

"Our openness and honesty
Will be the difference between...
...doing things With each other,
& being really With each other
doing things."

We are only children once ...

...but we can keep the child in us forever.

"... so often
we

spend so long
to look our best
to take our dog
for a walk ...

... and everyone comments
on what a beautiful dog
we have."

"... i want to talk with you
        to understand how you feel ...
... not to try to make you feel
        the way i do."

"... in words,
          i can share what i'm feeling ...
... in silence,
          i can feel what 'we're' sharing."

"... i hope you feel
        that i'm touching you
            with 'feeling',
        and not just to feel."

"i hope i appreciate what i have,
and don't take for granted
    what others would give anything for ...
... but most of all
    i hope i strive to do the most
        with all i have been given."

..."when i speak
    i'm saying
        what i already know,
when i listen
    i want to know
        more than i'm able to say...
...when i argue
    i need to be right,
when i discuss
    i want to share ...
... i hope my desire to love,
    is stronger than my need
        to be right."

"... the more open we are
        the less we seem strangers ...
... i've known people i've just met
        better than some people
        i've known for years ...
... i've known people
        who i've become strangers with ---

        ... i just hope
                we're always open ...

--- you're too precious to be a stranger."

"... you can hurt me
    by 'making others aware'
        of my mistakes ...
... you can help me
    by 'making me aware'
        of my mistakes ...
... your caring can inspire me
    to 'grow more aware'
        because of my mistakes."

"what a beautiful feeling to see...

        ...an elderly couple

      walking hand~in~hand,

      with sparkles in their eyes,

      and warm, gentle smiles...

at first,

    i 'only' saw that they were elderly...

then,

    i no longer saw what i had

    at first 'only' seen."

"I may not like
    what someone does,
but i love that someone
    Who does it."

- The child in us all -

I saw people gathered around a little baby, touching and hugging, and saying "what a beautiful baby!"

Then I looked around at everyone and saw that we were all once babies and said "what beautiful people!"

"if i touch you ?
    you'd rather i didn't
    'please' don't be afraid to tell me...
if i'm touching you for you,
    then i'll appreciate you telling me...
if i'm touching you for me,
    then i need to be told ---
        ... then ...
--- when we love
        with our touch,
    we'll be touched
        by our love."

"... you don't think you're special
   because i say nice things
   to a lot of people ...
When you think it's beautiful
   that i say nice things to others
   you will become more special."

"... i want a holiday so i can come back
and do something about the situations
i need a holiday from ...
... i don't want a holiday just to have
a rest and come back to the situation
so i'll need another holiday."

Silent Caring...

...if i'm sad about something
    and you don't know what to say,
please don't say anything...
    ...you'll say so much more.

"... i'm not afraid
        of 'growing old' ...
... i'm excited
        about 'growing'
            as i get older."

"... by being willing
      to take the risk
         to be different,
we may find that 'deep down'
      we are all the same...
... by trying
      to be the same
      we are often afraid
         of those
who may 'appear' different."

"My painful experiences can be positive
as they can make me a deeper
and more understanding person;
My beautiful experiences are positive
and they give me extra strength and
faith to face my painful experiences.
If i avoid having painful experiences,
i seem to lose the beautiful ones...
...and my spirit s.l.o.w.l.y d.i.e.s.

"... there , there ...
    ... don't cry "...

... tears are so real ...

... that's probably why
    we hide when we cry ...

... a fear of being close.

"How can you care about others,
     if you don't care about yourself;
and if you don't care about yourself,
     how can you expect others to care about you.

The more you take care of yourself,
     the more you'll care about yourself,
     the more you'll care about others,
     and the more others will care about you."

"... since i changed thinking
    that i can change others,
        i've changed ...
... and since i've changed,
    i think my thoughts
        have inspired others
            to change their thinking."

"... the more i've faced my fears
by being open ...
... the more my openness has brought
out others' fears."

"...If you 'love' someone
you want to understand them,
and you accept wherever they are...

...If you 'want' someone
you only accept them
if they are where you are,
or where you want them to be."

"...It's easy to love those
    who are the most loving...
... but what about those
    who need love most?"

"... it's simple to say
     beautiful things about someone
     when they aren't there ...
... but it's beautiful to say
     such simple things to someone
     as "i really do care".

"... Why do we argue over
        the silliest 'little things'?

        ... maybe because we aren't
really listening to each other ¿
what we are really saying ...

        ... this is a 'big thing'."

"... i may not be able
        to change the world i see
            around me ...
but ...
    i can change the way
        i see the world,
            within me."

"We are given so much with
the gift of life,
And with this gift we can
give so much to others."

"Birthdays ...
      ... ¦ other special occasions :~

   ... today,
         is special to you ...
   ... every day,
         you are special to me."

... i like
         your presents ...
but,
   ... i love

      your presence."

"... because i've been
            given a lot ...
... i've got to give
            all i've got."

"If you have something nice to say about me,
    please say it to me now while I'm alive and need it,
        not when it's too late and I'm gone."

"... When i'm infatuated,
     i 'only see'
          how good-looking someone is...

     ¿ then i 'hope'
          they're a beautiful person...

... When i'm loving,
     i 'see only' the beauty
          within someone...

     ¿ it doesn't matter
       how they look."

"if you'd 'just try' to understand
        Why i'm leaving you...
... i'd probably end up
        not leaving you."

"...Love
        is in our hearts,
and can be expressed
        thru our heads...
...our 'fears'
        develop in our heads,
and prevent us
        from being close
        to our hearts."

"... our love depends on
our openness to caring,
& our carefulness in being open...

... the depth of the love we share
depends on our equal openness
to care."

"...No,

i'm not quitting...

...i'm going to do something else."

"... i think it's right for me
    to belong to something
        if it always teaches me to love...
... i hope it's not
    'the belonging' that i love...

    as it might make me think
                i'm always right
    and those who don't belong,
            are wrong."

"... so often
we stay together
not for what we have,
but for what
we are afraid of losing...
--- if we'd appreciate
what we have,
it would only be
our fears
that we'd be losing."

"... when i `forgive´,
    i'm freeing myself to love
        at that moment in my life...
... when i `forget that i forgave´,
    i'm filling my life
        full of those moments...

... if i'm here `for giving´...
        ... i'll be getting,
if i'm here `for getting´...
        ... i hope i'll be forgiven."

"What are you going to be
     When you grow up?...

... i'm already 'being' now"

..."are you saying that
        because you really feel that way,
   or because others have told you
        that's the way you should feel?"

"... if we spend so much time trying to get a tan, buying clothes, putting on makeup, pumping iron, & styling our hair ...

... why do we give others such a cold & dirty look when they smile at us & say hello?"

"...If you won't be honest with me
because you're worried
about hurting me...
...you'll hurt me so much more
if i find out
you were dishonest."

"i'm not going,
        to leave you...
...i'm leaving,
        to go find me."

"...one of the most beautiful things about you is your warmth & love for people ...
    ... it's what attracted me to you;
    ... it's what the world really needs;
    ... it's what makes you so 'special'...

    ... i hope i always encourage, & not try to possess, the love you have for people & life ...

        ... it will make our relationship 'special'."

" ... in 'Wanting',
        i give to receive ...
... in 'loving',
        i receive from giving "

"... i saw a group of blind people
crossing the street,
    helping each other,
        laughing, ¿
            openly showing warm feelings
towards each other ...
... they were all different
        ages, colors, ¿ styles of dress...
... it didn't seem to influence
    their caring for each other ...

... i couldn't help wondering
    `who` is really blind."

"I'd rather be seen for who i am
and be alone,
than be accepted for someone i'm not
and be lonely."

"i didn't write these thoughts,
      so you'll feel
      i've written a beautiful book...
i've written this book,
      so you'll feel 'your beauty'
      with each thought."

with love always,
Brook Tully

... distributed by Simon & Schuster
(Green Tiger Division)
1 (800) 223 - 2336 (U.S.)
General Publishing
(416) 445 - 3333 (Canada)

☺ ~ a list of special books ~ ☺

~ "Living, Loving, ¿ Learning" ~ Leo Buscaglia
~ "Love" ~ Leo Buscaglia
~ "Illusions" ~ Richard Bach
~ "Jonathan Livingston Seagull" ~ Richard Bach
~ "The Elephant Man" ~ Ashley Montagu
~ Gandhi ~ any books by him or about him.
~ "The Prophet" ~ Kahlil Gibran
~ "The Little Prince" ~ Antoine de Saint Exupery
~ "The Wind in the Willows" ~ Kenneth Grahame
~ "The Velveteen Rabbit" ~ Margery Williams
~ "Love is Letting Go of Fear" ~ Gerald Jampolsky
~ "Teach only Love" ~ Gerald Jampolsky
~ "Strength to Love" ~ Martin Luther King, Jr.
~ "Siddhartha" ~ Hermann Hesse
~ "Winnie-the-Pooh" ~ A.A. Milne
~ "Notes to Myself" ~ Hugh Prather
~ "On Death and Dying" ~ Elizabeth Kubler-Ross
~ Mother Teresa ~ any books by her or about her works.
~ Jon-Lee Kootnekoff ~ hasn't written one yet ☺
~ "Women Who Love Too Much" ~ Robin Norwood